TRADITIONAL & POPULAR
WEDDING MUSIC COLLECTION

Here, in one book, are the most popular songs and traditional music celebrating love and marriage including Bridal Chorus, Canon in D, To Make You Feel My Love, Lovin' You, and the Wedding March. An audio Compact Disc of the backing tracks of each song is included.

CD Credits:
David Pearl—keyboards and arrangements
Ed Lozano—guitars
Peter Pickow—guitars, ukulele, lapsteel
Conrad Korsch—bass
Steve Holloway—drums

Produced by David Pearl, Ed Lozano, and Peter Pickow

Cover photography by Hope Reynolds of Hope Reynolds Photography

Order No. AM 948937
US International Standard Book Number: 0.8256.1712.X
UK International Standard Book Number: 0.7119.7592.2

Exclusive Distributors:
Music Sales Corporation
257 Park Avenue South, New York, NY 10010 USA
Music Sales Limited
8/9 Frith Street, London W1V 5TZ England
Music Sales Pty. Limited
120 Rothschild Street, Rosebery, Sydney, NSW 2018, Australia

Printed in the United States of America by
Vicks Lithograph and Printing Corporation

Amsco Publications
New York/London/Paris/Sydney/Copenhagen/Madrid

Track	Title	Page

Wedding March

Felix Mendelssohn

Bridal Chorus

Richard Wagner

CODA

D.S. al Coda

I'll Always Love You

Words and Music by Jimmy George

Lyrics:
1. I'll al - ways love you
2. love you
3. *Instrumental solo*

Two Tickets To Paradise

Words and Music by Eddie Money

Hawaiian Wedding Song

By Charles King, Dick Manning and Al Hoffman

I Love You Truly

Traditional, Arranged by David Pearl

Lovin' You

By Minnie Riperton and Richard Rudolph

Slowly, with expression

Lov - in' you is eas - y 'cause you're beau - ti - ful,

Mak - in' love with you is all I wan - na do.

Superstar

Words and Music by Bonnie Sheridan and Leon Russell

Moderately slow

That's How Strong My Love Is

Words and Music by Roosevelt Jamison

love is. Is- n't it? That's how strong

my love is, dar - ling, that's how strong my love is. A- gain now!

That's how strong my love is, so deep and

wide. That's how strong my love____ is.____

To Make You Feel My Love

Words and Music by Bob Dylan

When the rain is blow - in' in your face, ___

And the whole world is on your case, ___

Cm/Eb   G/D

(And) I could hold you for a mil - lion years ____

A7   D7sus4   G

To make you feel my love. ____

C   G

I know you have - n't made your mind up yet, ____

The storms are rag - ing on the roll - in' sea, ____

B7   C   G   Am/G G

But I would nev - er do you wrong.

And on the high - way of re - gret.

The Water Is Wide

Traditional, Arranged by David Pearl

Canon In D

By Johann Pachelbel
Arranged by David Pearl

Andante (♩ = 72)